# From Root to Seed: Black, Brown, and Indigenous Poets Write the Northeast

*From Root to Seed: Black, Brown, and Indigenous Poets Write the Northeast*
Edited by Samaa Abdurraqib, PhD

Published by NatureCulture LLC
www.nature-culture.net
www.writingtheland.org

ISBN:978-1-7375740-6-4
Library of Congress Control Number: 2023936470

Cover Artwork: *Barn Owl* by Martin Bridge
www.thebridgebrothers.com

Cover and Interior book design: Lis McLoughlin, PhD

¤
Related Volumes:
*Writing the Land: Currents* (2023)
*LandTrust* Poems by Katherine Hagopian Berry (2022)
*Writing the Land: Foodways and Social Justice* (2022)
*Writing the Land:Windblown I* (2022)
*Writing the Land:Windblown II* (2022)
*Writing the Land: Maine* (2022)
*Writing the Land: Northeast* (2021)
*Honoring Nature* (2021)

Series/related books publishers: 2022 & 2023 NatureCulture LLC
2021 Human Error Publishing
For more information: www.nature-culture.net

# From Root to Seed

Edited by Samaa Abdurraqib, PhD

Published by
NatureCulture LLC
Northfield, MA

## This Nature....It is Us.
## A Foreword by Shanta Lee

When I met this book, I did not realize that I'd been preparing for it for years: an interview with artist, storyteller and author, Dr. Carolyn Finney; and my work with the first known African American Poet, Lucy Terry Prince.

These verses stand in their power because they join their kin within a growing literary canon. *Black Nature: Four Centuries of African American Nature Poetry*, (Ed. Camille Dungy, 2009), was the first of its kind focusing on the nature writing of Black poets. *From Root to Seed*, reminds, instructs, and hands down a wisdom that echoes as strong as Courtney Lindwall's piece (2021, Natural Resources Defense Council), "Black Walden Came First. Thoreau, After."

The wisdom simply requires that one adjust their eyes, ears and whole spirit to take this in: The land so intimate, entangled with, kinned with Brown and Black Bodies that there is no true beginning or end as they have imprinted upon each other through time in ways that can't be counted.

An intimacy that predates the current revisitation; that supersedes any titles or words for the people who are entered into this kind of relationship; that embodied intersectionality because this marriage, this weddedness, this kinship go back to a before time.

And because of the degree of intimacy that Black and Brown bodies hold with the land, we are inviting you to reconfigure your seeing.

What you hold in your hands is many things all at once.

It is an invitation that invites you to see how the coastline, the trees, their roots, and all of the things within the landscape are aptly noticed as within Abdurraqib's verses they are "congregation/Spirit work" that brings you into a realm of the sacred that is just nature doing what it does.

It is a time-endured lullaby that lies within Doyon's verses "Every living thing began inside this same salty,/undulating womb, and every living thing must/ find its way back here, sometimes. Even you."

It is a chant with many things that invite repeating like within Russell's poem, "How long til I remember/this body belongs everywhere/on land/on sea/On Goddx, trust yourself to remember/to belong everywhere your ancestors have been/and everywhere future kin have yet to see"

It is the reminder that land can be the site of crimes within the enmeshment with Black and Brown Bodies, e.g. Jordan-Zachery's "Break, in case of emergency" with the lines "The sea ain't got no back door!"

And a reminder about the vanished points between nature, humanity and harm within Hardy's lines, "The priest contemplates murder    red    rain amphibians    boils    slick/ swords    calls these plagues.//But then there are the murders/of everything black. Everybody./ Everyone sees this."

*From Root to Seed* is also a clear road mapped toward an imprinting within your own spirit in three sections, that when put together in one full bodied line, speak as a full verse and summoning.

A Place            For Our Bodies            In These Surroundings

The spellwork is the verses that invite you to do a noticing while you allow yourself to become engaged in an undeniable seduction and destruction that is what we want to stamp as the wild as if we are separate from it. However, what these poets remind us is that the concept of separation is impossible just as undeniable as the woven fact of violence, death, beauty and just-is-ness that is nature itself/ourselves.

A welcome is equally important as a good-bye. In *From Root to Seed,* you are properly greeted with the first instruction that is Montgomery's poem about allowing the things around us to be the guide, inviting you, your spirit and your whole mind to engage with a coming home of sorts while Paul's closing poem tells it in the final lines, "Live as you are meant to live./Live./Live."

In an era when living Black and Brown is an audacious act, how could we not listen as these lines instruct? How can we not do the doin?

Nature does what it does and so shall we in our kinning with it.

Come in, as this does not require you know how to read a field guide. Come in, as this does not require that you have to language right in order to take it in. You don't need to know the latin names for things that have had names long before someone decided to up and name them.

Enjoy the verses.
Taste them in your mouth.
Feel them as you feel all that holds you.

This land. This Nature that is us and we are it.

## Preface: A Place for Our Bodies in These Surroundings

When you think about the land and the ecosystem of the Northeastern region of the United States, what do you imagine? You likely envision the rolling hills and mountains of the places we now call New Hampshire, Vermont, and Maine. You might imagine coastlines – both rocky cliffs and sandy beaches. Perhaps you visualize wide open spaces in the north and densely congested spaces in the south and west of the region. And when you think of Black, Brown, and Indigenous people in the region, where do you place us? Are we in those wide-open spaces? Are we in engaging with the natural world or are we set apart and isolated from it?

*Dear reader, I need to tell you: we are everywhere. And we are in relationship with the land and with nature wherever we are.*

The ways that we relate to nature are as diverse as we are – from cookouts in the city park, to through-hiking the Appalachian trail, to mastering horticulture. Personally, I found my way into a conscious relationship with nature in my mid-30s. This relationship grew from a place of necessity – a need for healing and a need to be grounded in something outside of myself. When I moved from the Midwest to the Northeast and into the land stewarded by the Wabanaki people, I found that healing and grounding in the breathtaking ecosystem of the region that begged me to stay. And so I did – I stayed.

As I fell deeper and deeper in love with the land and its non-human inhabitants, I was confronted with the idea that my Black body did not belong in these wide-open spaces. At times this message would resound loud and clear in the questions about my presence at a bird sanctuary or doubt cast towards my skills and expertise. But, more often, I found the message in the absences. When I would go out exploring, I rarely saw people who looked like me. When I would take courses or go on naturalist-led educational walks, I rarely saw people who looked like me. When I would search the wealth of ecopoetry or nature poetry coming from this region for voices that sounded like mine, I rarely found them.

*From Root to Seed* speaks volumes into that void. The poets featured in this collection situate themselves firmly in the Northeast and put themselves in conversation with the land they know and the natural world they celebrate.

The poems in the section "A Place" give shape to land and to place, both the at-home feelings connected to place as well as the feelings of disconnection and rejection. Framed by Jason Montgomery and Robert Anthony Gibbons pausing and opening themselves up in awareness to the beacons in nature that call and speak to us. Throughout this section, the poets grapple with the power of stones, the ocean, and the perpetual harms colonizers have inflected on Black, Brown, and Indigenous people who have called these lands home.

From the macro-view to the micro-view, "For Our Bodies," turns attention to Black, Brown, and Indigenous bodies inhabiting the natural world and contending with all it has to offer. From Rheros Iliad Kagoni's brief meditation on their likeness to strawberries to Mihku Paul's wading in to greet the "congregation of pebbles" and the life below the water, this section reminds us that non-white bodies have always had a place in and intimate understanding of the natural world.

"In These Surroundings" draws our attention back out, outside of ourselves and beyond land. The poems in this section engage on the level of ecosystem, grappling with the waiting and loss wrapped up in phenology and the passing of time. The poems in this section are rife with weighty contemplations, like RescuePoetix's questioning our interpretation of star language and Ebbie Russell's woeful call to the woods of Plainfield, "Who will hold me when I return?"

This collection is important because it responds, with resonance: YES, we are here. Through resistance and resilience, we are here. With our deep-rooted knowing and our mutli-faceted understanding of this land, this place, and our connections – we *are* here and we *have been* here.

—*Samaa Abdurraqib, PhD*
*Brunswick, Maine*
*April 2023*

# Table of Contents

## A Place

# For Our Bodies

# In These Surroundings

# A Place

# A Nonet for Charlestown, RI
Jason Montgomery

There are lights floating on night insects
Lights drifting like clouds on the sea
There are lights across the sky
of lights there are many
along the shores of
Charlestown's night
All of which
guide me
home.

## Ode to Sarah Baartman
Dylan Richmond

My dreams are filled with boats and
our mother—
      diamond, coffee, ivory, freedom—
filling the ocean with salt as she weeps.

      The lamentations grow thunderous.
      These are (not) my memories.

There are two continents
I know:
      America,
      my body.
      You have colonized both.

It is no wonder clouds darken before they rain tears—
they are starting to feel more like us.

The petrichor comes first.
Utnapishtim, tell again how it was done.
The torrent takes me
      like a lover; in the riptide, (your)
Venus is swung into detriment.

Floodgates agape,
(I think) I see the
      nape of god.

Soon I am only and ever osmosis.

I am not afraid of drowning;
      it is my comfort. Civil,
the sharks must remember me.
      Perhaps the soil of my skin,
      the choir in my screams.

I am a strangled hymn,
the dissonance

resolution.

**James Baldwin on Madison Avenue**
Robert Anthony Gibbons

I walked up Madison near the antiquarian book shop you know, one of those
stores that are used to preserve the rare and antique, the oddity and unique,
and there he was in the window, the preacher's son of Harlem

wrapped in the swaddling clothes of preservation paper, sorry Baldwin, I can't
afford the ink, can not afford, the taking and pillaging, for I am everybody's
protest novel, hobbling up Madison, near the Frick

full of Piero's and Bruncusi's, full of Miro's and Raushenberg's. I am still in
tenement form, a gray shutter with a storm drain, so I pick up my dignity and
call it elegy call it death to the salesman, with all these railroad

apartments, these pseudo-benefactors and latch keys to culture, Baldwin, I
have fallen under the spell of your Renaissance, there is no celebration of color
in preservation paper the protest is still a hoax, there are more artifacts to
come from the civil rights

so I ended my journey in the library with a little brown box that said free
books and one that was left was going to meet the man.

## Late Autumn Observing The Coastline of Beals Island
Samaa Abdurraqib

Where the rocky coastline meets the forest,
there are places where the roots of trees

cling to boulders, twisting and joining,
threading themselves through one another.

I want to call this a congregation.

A place of testifying to strength and the near
impossibility of roots siphoning water from stones.

Spirit-work.

No matter how tall or keeled over by the elements,
roots join, knuckle to knuckle, telling stories of

erosion and of days past. Of the shoreline that
used to be, crumbled. Of the legs of relatives who

used to stride and skirt the edges, vanished now.
Tree limbs and arms thrust high-high,

fingers bare, tense and taught, fanning out in all
directions, like a scene of liberation.

I want to call this a ululation.

A moment of lifting up in praise and shaking off when
the winds barrel through and say it is time.

Sacrificial.

To give up all adornment and color and to be seen,
vulnerable in praise, fully open in adoration.

Of themselves. Of each other.

**Preserve the Pure**
Nourish Cruz
Location:  *Seeley's Pond, Watchung Reservation*

I know every tree like family
tripped stone as stranger
hold a flower like a clover
in a sea of 3.

I dance along the water
it waves back.
Catch a shimmy on a fishing line.
Hook my eyes onto the edge of the fall.

I cleanse my feet
from pavement to pond.
I steal a little earth in my shoes.
It makes my smile pure.

Turtle!

Childlike, age is forgotten here.
Sun rays fill wrinkles.
Broken branches fly as high as birds.
I whistle like them.

Never mind a mosquito out of key.
Never mind the dog barking, after the squirrel.
Never mind the faint call of the steel jaguar
across the street.

Wait, who left a wrapper on the grass?

**Land**
Deidra Suwanee Dees

stretching my arms,
            cool Charles River air entered
my mouth,

just finished
writing a
kick-ass article exposing the
            evils of stolen Massachusetts
            land through
            assimilation;

live oaks reverberated,
            *"asssssssimilation—*
            if Natives had not
learned to
assimilate,

you would not exist on this land";

troubled, wondering,
            "did assimilation *save us?*"

rewriting
            the
            article

## Break, in case of emergency
Julia S. Jordan-Zachery

"The sea ain't got no back door!" My father often warned.
His way of telling me that it will let me in
but not necessarily back out.
Its unpredictable hum,
an alarm of terrible and unfathomable chaos.

With the churning of the ocean, boulders replace seashells.
Waves, once gentle, become impatient and powerful.
Chaos, rumbling at the bottom.

Days later, the earthquake would hit.
Haiti.
Devastated again!

Chaos, tumultuous and murky, fills spaces.
Chaos, dark and deep like the ocean, vibrating.
Chaos, with a pounding and steady rhythm, like the waves lapping against the
shore, crushes.

The shore eroded over time as we dump what we no longer need into the sea.
Leaving it uncared for as we frolic, sunbathing, and,
marveling at its majesty.

Seashells once lay freely on the sand,
their melody, eclectic,
blends to create a brief but melodious tune
in concert with the swollen amber sun.
They offer a prophetic call,
seemingly unheard by us who roam the shore in search of solace.

Hypnotic and seemingly peaceful, chaos lurking at the bottom.
Reverberating,
letting us in, but never back out.

### The Path to Heaven is by Lifeboat
Maya Williams

You may not have all your Christian ducks in a row,
but you have your Protestant hopes for the afterlife. in a row.
You don't know if it's correct to say you were Agnostic about heaven six
years in a row,

but you do know Grief makes you believe in heaven and
swim to lifeboat
carry all your loved ones. oh so gently.
Pray and hold An ocean of sky up
and down

swooping souls to heaven's waiting room. It gives you comfort.
The

Freezing body of water stream
frames of discount Jesuses.
Merrily

your soul thriving, walking, strolling up Capisic
Pond. Merrily

acknowledging in ethereal gray and
white. Merrily

your body alive and exhaling fog. Merrily
grateful for this soul, this breath, this one
life,

trying your damnedest— *your blessedest* is
what Grandma Reece would prefer— to get right. But
you may not always get it right; a priceless Jesus is only
a dream.

## Eighty-Six
Deidra Suwanee Dees

three sixty-six busses stacked up against
each other,
butt to nose, engines idling,
an "out of service" arrogantly whizzes by
as my body feints forward; taunting me;
*where the hell is eighty-six?*

cold wind walks its way up
my pants legs and three layers of shirts,
freezing torso, trying to get to
Indigenous Studies at Harvard; not
this cold back home in Alabama;
*where the hell is eighty-six?*

feet no longer stomping—heavy blocks of
ice; deadened
fingers, wind-chill tears;
*where the hell is eighty-six?*

hood taking on snow—*I think I see it!*
I think it's here—it looks like eighty-six!
*daaaamn!* it's another sixty-six

## pale stones: a triptych
*after French Falls*
Ian-Khara Ellasante

**1.**
river water rushing over pale stones
and deep human breaths in place
i take note of   the human
the compulsion to claim
the compulsion to place   a self
myself   here
the compulsion to name   the place
in time   of my arrival
as if it matters
the human hand   i place
riverside   flat against a pale stone
steadying   *this is the anchor* i tell   myself
relieved   though perhaps i believe that i am
the real anchor: the human   has placed
a self here   named and renamed
      and remained
in a jumble of moss-laden pale stones
trundled halfway down a hillside
a stenciled sign   a declaration: PYLOROX
      and remained
between a pair of trees   a station for sitting
nail and hammer secured   a bench
a stenciled sign   an invitation: HAVASEET
      and remained
in the eleven planks of a foot bridge
in all the markers   signaling   the human
access and acquaintance:
this is birch  and this is red maple  that is
red oak   and a guide to the habits
dietary and otherwise   of the porcupine
the life cycle of the field mouse
the predation of the bald eagle   a guide
to the boot-pounded path   a guide

to the color-flagged trail  marking the falls
a place   where the river does
something more impressive
than simply plunge itself infinitely
forward   its constant state constant
     changing
moment to moment  a place
named for what
these pale stones can make a river do


**2.**
pale stones   slabbed and scattered
set down with the resolve of millennia
laid here by the will of earth's wise body
pale stones   over which a river hurtles
into the gravity of a subtle cascade
pale stones   over which a river drapes a veil
darkening them into water's wet shade

pale stones   a river   and a human
                    existing by chance  here
                            for a moment  here
by happenstance  i find myself here

*which of us is the anchor?*
i ask these stones   i ask the river
as i capture and claim   images of them
as i capture
as i claim   as i walk away

this impulse   is it in my blood
     human that i am  my blood
laced with settler
blood draping a veil over pale stones
darkening their faces   pale stones
once barrier   once obstacle
now smoothed

into a type of submission
slowly becoming silt in my veins


**3.**
it's been said before    from the desert
in which rivers unwind themselves
underneath the earth
i said it a decade ago    said it from the dry desert
said sometimes the changes in a river's course are scars

and now  so far from the desert
from here  where water
manifests each season  changing
and changes the saturated earth
where the river goes through and throughout
where lush layers of forest nestle against its banks
where the river falls infinitely upon itself
where a name is not what i call myself
it is what and who i am
where a name for this place and others
falls short  of resemblance   of reckoning

sometimes the changes to a river's course
are a collection of scars    still true and
sometimes the changes to a river's course
are a collection of pale stones
            slowly becoming silt


N.B. "pale stones: a triptych" by Ian-Khara Ellasante was first published in
*Writing the Land: Maine* (Northfield, MA: NatureCulture) 2022.

# a crooked tree on Carol Street, Brooklyn, New York City
Robert Anthony Gibbons

a perfect day for a crooked tree
an examination of the eyes
the rumination of the wise
maybe the street is canopy

aligned with liability
she wants light
so, she searches every corner
every chapter, every verse

till she covers Earth
her stubborn worth, maybe
she seeks clarity
if she's headstrong

I am wrong
it's she,
the tree decides
to lean and stick her chest out

maybe she's a feminist
with all her varicose
and blemishes
it's hard being stable

when life is not always arable
so, I'll admire her monument
her tries and rudiments
as I walk away up Carol Street

this one crooked tree
speaks to me

# For Our Bodies

## Eu Sou Capoeira
Winston Antoine

I am a Capoeirista
I wonder what it means to be balanced
I hear the vibrations of the berimbau hum through the air
I see the spirits of my ancestors in the joda
I want to learn and teach, I want to learn to teach
I am a Capoeirista

I pretend to be the animals that surround me
I feel the energy of the environment
I touch the ground in homage of those before me, those that support me
I worry about passing it on
I cry at my physical and mental limitations
I am a Capoeirista

I understand that I am the sum of many wholes
I say that true beauty is shown under the sway of the moonlight
I dream about Calypso and me, the flow of the sea
Try to see the Ocean in me
I am a Capoeirista

## Strawberries Pt. 2
Rheros Iliad Kagoni

Strawberries always look better than they taste.
Never as sweet as I would like,
bitter against my tongue
I imagine that I am like that,
good from a distance
bitter if you're too close.
When I say she looks like
Someone who loves the taste of strawberries
I am talking about the sweet ones.

She loves me, she loves me not.
The roots that I cut were never meant to regrow
She loves me, she loves me not
Bitter strawberries on a summer day
She loves me, she loves me not
I'll learn to love strawberries for her.

**elsewhere**
Ian-Khara Ellasante


.i.

from
the dry desert  i call forth
the weeping  the weary
the soggy geography
of mississippi delta
rivers like creases
pressing into her flat palm
from
the desert   i write to
the delta       i write to
the bottom of a heart
from
the lonely desert  i write a conjure
where thirsty rivers sink
into sun-baked dust
i ache for my grandmothers
mamoun and grandmama and all
the seen and the shadows
the felt and forgotten
the long gone    the living on
*give me your names*
i write  i whisper in unbroken undulation
*grandmothers  tell me my names*
*to help me see my face*
*you are unraveling and home*
*is burning a path in me*
*grandmothers  give me your names*
*are you there?*
*home is burning  she's burning down*


.ii.

here
an ocean unfolds itself  toward me
stretches to meet the rivers halfway

and i bear a child
seven miles from the sea
          here
as a dark winter curls away
like the bark of yellow birch
spring slips new velvet
slivers of day into the start
and the end of each night
here     in this dawnland
i birth a child
one ray of light   and another
first-born daughter
of our grandmothers' long lines
          our hands and wombs
          all knit together
          though their hearths
          and names remain  lost to me
          a home   turns in to me
          a home   falls away from me
then this child comes from me
     she knows her own name
     she knows
          and home comes to me
          here
i birthed this daughter    and now
i dream of shortcuts to mamoun's front door
of turns and paths    i never saw before
i birthed a daughter here   and now
i dream of the homes i thought i knew
houses with whole other houses
hidden within

.iii.
my child reaches a dimpled hand
to greet spruce tips and moss
ancient stone and beach sand
lake ripples   and mirrors her laughter
as a blue heron wades at water's edge

she presses her fingers  into my palm
to melt the snow    i have gathered
for her    here
crows call and she knows where to look
leaves fall and crunch underfoot
at every step with her here
roots burrow deep beneath my soles
i cradle her feet in my hands

*may you always know your way home*

## Medicinal Eclipse
Samara Cole Doyon

When I was 36 years old,
I learned that blocking out the sun,
sometimes, can be a blessing,
a poultice you spread softly over yourself.

You pull close the curtains, a blanket,
gathering thunderclouds to your face;
Drop raised palms, welcome softly
thick air swallowing lashes, limbs;
Sink beneath the dark brine
gathering on your skin, flowing steadily,
instinctively downward, to sea level;

To reclaim your birthright—time and space;
breath and blood—as you sometimes must,
you must sometimes block out the sun.
It is not the end, but the rhythm of all things,
rising and falling inside you as it must.

Every living thing began inside this same salty,
undulating womb, and every living thing must
find its way back here, sometimes. Even you.

# The power of the people the color of the earth
Joy George

The power of the people the color of the earth
Comes from our magic and skillfulness in disruption
So much so
That the ones who came to conquer us called our tricker gods "the Devil"
And our medicine women "witches"

They could not fathom how our sovereign knowing ran so deep

And so,
They planted seeds to destroy and divide us—
Sought to remove us from our lands and force us to forget the ancestors buried there

In every year, the dead of winter rolls forward into spring,
And with it comes the thawing of the soil
Every year, the full blooms of summer rolls forward into the sweet smell of autumn decay

Our knowing is so deep because our people organize on earth time

We organize at the pace of shedding layers, transformation, regeneration and divine timing

We are never too far from home
Our ancestors live on in our bones and gut-brains
Waiting to be conjured
Patiently anticipating their time to return

They return, in bold revolution, at the time when the light is returning
And the earth decrees "NO MORE!"

"These systems are dying" they whisper
"It is now your time to rise and remember. Come home."

Those who came to conquer us did not anticipate our defiance

That in our survival, we would be home no matter where we were

Those who came to conquer us would be
BIG MAD,
VIOLENT,
PUSH BACK,
WHITE HOODED,
LASH OUT,
REDLINING

It would not matter.

We would bring our homes into spaces that were unfamiliar to our spirits,
Through Afrobeats, and words spoken of jollof and blessed oil
So that that the rhythms and scents of our legacy
Would fill up the emptiness and call the egungun to be present

We would become beacons calling to those who would next arrive

We would be home in the ways our heads carried high above our shoulder,
Crowning straight backs,
Withstanding and exceeding expectations with the confidence of
Chiefs and lolos,
Dibias and land-tenders,
Unbothered because our people no dey carry last oooo

We would be home amongst the trees,
Alongside the riverbanks,
And on top of mountains
Because we know how to honor a divinity when our own meet another

We would become the healers our bloodlines needed,
Re-membering, re-engaging, re-aligning

We would be home when we meet our kindred across the diaspora spread far
and wide,
Dandelion seeds in a westward wind,
Recognizing our Selves in theirs:

The beauty of our mirrored dances,
The likeness in our voiced expressions:
We are home in the wide global net that is the true majority

We are home in the calm knowing that these systems are empty, designed poorly,
And dying a natural death,
Watching with simple smiles in the wings

Because eventually, we will be home because all that will be left is us

Once again, we will have survived

Coaxing, nurturing, tending, teaching, marching, resisting, building

Practicing our values through the power in our tongue and the sovereignty of our collective body

It is safe for us to speak,
And know that our existence is valid

We know deeply
We know deeply
We know deeply

The power of the people the color of the earth comes from our tenacity to thrive:
In any soil.

## Pandemic Walk With a Forester Friend
JuPong Lin

Six feet-ish apart we hug
our own bodies, yearning for each
others arms. Past the playground
she's known since childhood,
we enter the trail, new to us both.
Julius Lester, the only black author
who got a trail named after him,
wrote dozens of children's books.
But the pictures and words that punctuate
the path now say nothing
of Julius, Br'er Rabbit, Br'er Fox
trickster lessons for surviving.

I spot horsetail by the brook.
We walk through a sawn down
birch, sickened by fungus.
She shows me the growths
pock marking the bark.
Death marks, making food
for new life.
We talk of broken marriages
repairing relationships,
breathe the moist air
together, wave
until our next
walk.

# Falling Backwards Through an Abundance, I Am
Samaa Abdurraqib

I fall backwards through an abundance of trees —
 spruce trees — some boughs pulling me back

the ones in front pushing me further in, I could
 feel the triple SSS of their needles pricking

punishment because I've made this mistake before
 and confused the species, expecting softness

where there is none, like when I told you that I
 was scared, there, under the water, and

you set your eyes firm as if to say, "you did not
 die," even though it felt just like an ending.

Arms outstretched with palms wide I grab hand-
 fuls with a satisfying snap as needles separate

fully from the base, I will save some needles for a
 satchel that I will tie closed and place in two

mugs of boiling water which we will swallow deeply
 to break up the cold and dispel the cough and

ward off the cancers, or so we've been told by the
 people who know best, people I would trust

to pull me up towards the surface before the water
 clogs my ears, enters my lungs, completely

saturates and distends me, their hands firmly in the
 crooks beneath my shoulders, their eyes direct &

soft as if to say, "we will not let you die here" in this
 muddy creek flanked by those who turn away.

Chin to chest, surrounded by an abundance of heavy
    scent, I stumble into a conflation and find myself

mistaking scent for cleanliness and I allow myself
    to fully relax into the spic and span of it all

the purification of pine and I close my eyes as I lay
    back into it all, knowing the needles and small

branches become bedding if placed just right and
    if belief and comfort are suspended for just a

night and I allow the scent to envelope me, carry
    me to a place that is firm and familiar like

this forest floor, where I can finally look lovingly
    at myself as if to say, "I refused to die there,"

in that muddy creek water, where my feet did not
    touch the bottom, surrounded by those who

turned away from my fear. Falling backwards through
    an abundance of pine, I am here, I am alive.

# Hawk with Crow

Myronn Hardy

The hawk holds the crow in talons.
The red maple is barren     holding them
both in boughs as crows gather.

Crows call     warn the hawk
of the danger arriving.
The danger the hawk inflicts on the crow.

Its beak through feathers     lava skin.
The plunging     how life is slowly purged.
The black of it     broken.

A hawk besotted by its slaughter
despite the now murder of crows
surrounding.

Despite the murder of crows
surrounding a man on a hill
because he ate one of them.

Roasted one of them
desperately with a potato     squash.
The priest knows of the murder.

The dark stones of the monastery know too.
All of the crows gathering     looking
at that man know.

Their darkness is his
darkness in that dark sky.
The priest says: *murder     murderer.*

Feathers swing from the murderer's mouth.
The hawk swings to the ground.
Two murders beneath that tree.

The priest contemplates murder     red
rain     amphibians     boils     slick
swords     calls these plagues.

But then there are the murders
of everything black.  Everybody.
Everyone sees this.

### If I Were a Rose.
Rheros Iliad Kagoni

I am sad to inform you that I am not a rose
Perhaps I am closer to a cactus.
I survive under the hot sun and
harsh environments that I have been placed in, against my will.
If you get close enough, you'll find,
Something worth your while inside,
Something to keep you alive and
Maybe, maybe it'll all be worth it
in the end, if you get close enough.
A cactus has more thorns than a rose
And I am afraid that I am not a rose,
And I hope you can ignore the blood on your hands,
Maybe if you can ignore the blood, if you just keep pushing,
Pushing through the thorns,
Towards the core, the center, the thing that really matters...
That's what I do.

A rose would be easier to present.
A rose would hide the blood better.
But I cannot change what I am,
And if there is too many thorns to remove
Maybe it'll still be worth your while
Anyhow.

**Water**
Brooke Bolduc

Together we share a divine dance
Your skin to mine, like the softness of water
Pooling over flesh, reaching every inch
I encourage you, I invite you.
Embrace me like you know I accept all of you.
Crash over me, engulf me, cradle me.
I offer you peace and serenity with every touch.
Like water.

Artwork: *Water* by Brooke Bolduc "Buff Cat"

## Etiquette for Beginners
Mihku Paul

When I wade in,
my giantess toes sink through
yellow sand, fallen twigs, leaves
in their dark decay.
Here and there a congregation of pebbles.
Only water dwellers and lake denizens
can truly know this place,
their intimate universe, home.
Below the surface horizon,
minnows dart and shimmer.
Sensing mass, movement, they race from
shapeless danger, instinct,
we name it.
Nature guides us all, if we are willing.
Her wisdom brutal, beautiful.
She asks only that we remember our place,
the gifts we are given.
And so these tiny fishes flee as
my pale feet plow forward,
harrow the soft bottom.
For me, a less obvious destruction,
nearly beyond my notice,
but not theirs.

## A place in nature, a place in a natural body
Ebbie Russell

Does it feel right?
Does it flow?
What odds
am I working against?
What do I know?
What can I trust myself
to remember?

Earlier this year
I remembered how to swim
while lying prone on the chiropractic table

      anchor
      boat
      buoy
      fish
      ship

An arrow twisting
afraid of stretching to the fullness
of my limbs

Must extend
Must unfurl
Must untangle the numerous dreams
in which I'm afraid of flying,
drowning

What shapes must I take of my marine
mammal ancestors?
How can I undulate the knots in my spine?
The twisting of my limbs?
How do I too learn breathing underwater?

How long til I remember
this body belongs everywhere

      on land
      on sea

On Goddx, trust yourself to remember
to belong everywhere your ancestors have been
and everywhere future kin have yet to see

**Untitled**
Sett Vincent

I have no problem with the sand, the seagulls -

　　　they overwhelm me, and make me afraid to eat my lunch.

I like the tan the sun gives me -

　　　actually, I miss it.

I love the bits of crab you can find sometimes -

　　　the gentle reminder that a body of bone and armor won't protect
you from the constant pecking of empty stomached birds.

I first left the concrete slabs unwillingly, trading them like my grandmother's
ring for moss and lakes -

　　　i was scared. my feet, until this point, were made for work boots
and highways.

I felt blind -

　　　like i couldnt see the mountain tops past the billboards, the bees
past the buzzing, the soil past the dirt.

I came to Maine, scared of the unknown, wondering what I could accomplish
in a state with more pine than people -

　　　i discovered poetry in the bark, oil pastel in the water, healing in
the people.

I found a home -

　　　one I didnt know was lost.

### Sparrow, 2018
Miriam Uduebor

New to this mainland, I feel silenced and unseen.
Newness leading to an immediate sense of loneliness.
Unknown to where to go
or who to seek.
Noticing that those who are bright in conversation,
immediately catch everyone's eyes and thus ears.

*Cardinals. Baltimore Orioles.*

Even those with just a pinch of colorful surprise
catch sights and chances for new adventures.

*Red winged blackbirds.*

But I, camouflaged in anonymity,
some brown bird over there,
is hidden easily amongst the barks and shadows of the lands around me.
And I, as I am, have no attractive tune to sing out a call
for connection.

**magic**
Dylan Richmond


when i was seven i believed i could speak to the ocean.
my name in welsh means born from the sea
and my magic is like water.

in all things with breath, it is there;
when i am there, it is drinking.

my ancestors know a lake named freedom—
it will never dry up.

> i fish there, and always throw back what I have caught.
> > would you?
>
> thrown back, i am both the ripple
> and what has caused the ripple.
> > are you?

when i come out of a river, standing still, i am moving.

when i step from the ocean and kiss you    softly    on the forehead,
the salt that remains will divulge you.

the salt that remains on me will kill.
and i will shed that skin and become new and clean.

if you have smelled the wind right before a storm, you have tasted my magic.
if you have smelled the wind following this storm, you have tasted my magic.

if you have opened your eyes underwater—
watched sunlight bend, felt skin rendered lighter than it has ever been.
watched gravity be deceived,        a love
              felt swim into you,        so deep.
        your body that love, your dancing how it tells the secret. have you
felt?
then you know my magic.

but you will never know my magic
because i can speak to the ocean
and it has told me

                "you are mine."

**Golden**
Samara Cole Doyon

I wish I could hide here forever
inside this mid-October afternoon
where I've found my heart beating again after all.

And the corn stalks in the maze stand golden
and the falling birch leaves tumble golden
and the aging sunlight slants golden
over everything, staining the world
in a golden-brown honey wash.
And the air is crisp and clean
as the languishing death of new beginnings.

And if I get lost alone in the corn maze after dark
and the lights go out, and if everyone goes home
without me, now, I won't be afraid
because I know that I know
that you will always come back for me
like painted skeleton leaves tumbling on the breeze
that blows through late afternoons in mid-October.

**Nasturtiums**
Myronn Hardy


The dew over pine fronds     the paper
of birches     that wet scent     alpine
we're staring at a pine cabin

we must leave.
We're telling it
*goodbye*     the land     the water     a kind of peace.

Goodbye to loss     the boulders
beneath our feet from which we slid.
Goodbye to placid water     how

it falls over us tenderly.
Our arms raised to it.
We were not raised here

but we've risen from sleep     from
babble     from languages we only know.
We've jumped into that warm

water despite that gelid air.
Something up from the water saying
something to us     something muted

something pale.
You point to the nasturtiums.
How beaten they look     how damp

yet protected by warily set stones.
We pluck the blossoms     taste
their pungency     their peculiar spice.

We're aware now.
We're open to the open.
We're alive.

# In These Surroundings

# While Driving on I-295
Maya Williams

I saw a beautiful brown hawk

gliding in mid-air.

I never saw one this close before.

Then, six feet below its flight,

I saw bloodied butchered pieces

of a deer upon the road.

Dammit. Mia was right.

I *can* see the bright side of roadkill.

I want to push out pessimism.

Prove them wrong.

But I can't.

Beauty was witnessed

and fed well.

## Winter of Resilience

Ashini J. Desai

I.
Frozen rain pelted the trees last winter.
We stayed inside our warm houses while the winds howled,
rattling the windows and chilling our bones.
Sharp slivers of drafts seeped through the windows that never closed properly.
The skies cast an eerie luminescence all evening.

II.
The mornings after always glistened. Sunlight sparkled
through the glassy icicles, projecting rainbows.
Leaves were swathed in ice.
We exhaled "A winter wonderland" when we saw
the white-capped pine trees lining the streets,
harkening collective memories of Currier & Ives.
The roads gleamed in the clear reflections of splendor.

III.
The series of crackles broke the silence of the frosty air.
Ice clung to the branches as the trees bowed unnaturally.
Some twisted spines to kneel on the ground, genuflecting with branches
sprawled.
Other trunks broke into clean planks in the middle
as heavy limbs hit the grass without a warning.

I cried when our large front tree could no longer endure the struggle,
surrendering its branches with loud snaps.
Some boughs were strewn across the yard
and others still cradled in the arms of another tree.

The men came with ladders, chainsaws, and the skills of acrobats
to tow the remains away.

IV.
When the air turned to warm and the sunshine lingered longer,
the trees rose from their bent stature. They stooped no more.

Once again, the graceful Leyland Cyprus stood upright.
The warmer breezes of April eventually coaxed the pear tree to blossom,
even fuller with new offshoots from the split limbs.
The white lilacs bloomed in June as always.

V.
I realized I had naively grieved for the trees,
as victims of nature's force, suffering a silent death.
Yet, it was only a quiet dormancy –
a contemplative state to heal and recover from the elements.
Like the trees, we bend and crack when we uphold an unnatural weight.
Our burdens fall when a part of us breaks.
We sit on our knees and wait.
Eventually we will stand upright and sprout supple green stems.

If we choose to observe,
the trees have silently taught us.

Release. Rise. Flourish.

**Methodology of Cardboard**
JuPong Lin

he sinks his hand into a deep, dark
layer of soil, lifts the blanket of decomposing
Cardboard, his face beaming with joy and love
for the lace woven by mycellia, the wiggly worms
and invisible microbial beings
all feeding the garlic, kale and chard
we will eat for lunch

she gathers us in a circle embracing
new regenerative friendships
tells a story of growing love
under the stars, growing a movement
of soil lovers, no-tillers seeding
good land relations
holding a vision of rematriating* land
in a palmful of earth.

we sing praises to cardboard,
permeable yet protective,
digestible shelter
Undisturbed, Earth returns to her
fertile, life-giving self.

* Ferreira, Celeste, et al. "Indigenous Women's Worldview in Food-Related
Research: Rematriating Food, Bodies and Lands." *Applied Physiology, Nutrition,
and Metabolism*, vol. 47, no. 2, Feb. 2022, pp. 210–13.

## When Stars Speak

RescuePoetix / Susan Justiniano

Tell me,
when the stars speak
what language do they use?

When they spell out realities
in ways that mean life
what alphabet burns across the sky?

Wait ...

The more critical question is:
Do you understand it?

When you look up and see the splaying
of light, do you take it for granted?
Expect it to be there night after night,
like a reoccurring dream?

Or

Do you take the twinkling to mean
an echo of the passion for reality
that so few of us truly embrace?

There's something to be said for
the black and white of facts

No judgment in truth

Truth is at a place where kindness
isn't even a factor
It just is

Spread out before us
in a pattern that we interpret

based on our perception

Those stars never truly change
the message is always the same
we read them how we want to see them

To be able to grasp their light
burn their stories in the palms of our hands
experience the lives that can burn out in an instant

How significant it is to remember them!
passed from generation to generation
hidden in songs that we no longer listen to

Look again

We are in each of those stars,
our stories, lifetimes of lives
spread out across universes of other lives

Speaking in ways, that, while some may not know
still burns bright
splayed across truth in the midnight meadow of light

## The Creator
Nourish Cruz

I make waves
before the moon beams

carve poems
into the wisdom tree.

I wake graves
to turn the soil
sow seeds with holy oil.

Make magnesium mountains
that can erupt interchangeably
into ethereal fountains.

Fault line
inner view of virtuous intention.

Understand how this sun can rise
without suspension.

I break days into snowflakes and stanzas
rest on the 7th syllable of a Haiku
create an Earth to say goodnight to.

## Elelogap
Crystal Davis

Water Spirit,
Sailing through the waters
Like a scaly sea dragon as
he shimmers
From sunlight's refraction.

Elevated through waves. Exalted
by the living waters. Praised by
the flowing river.
Running deep within the celestial ocean.

He governs the rain, the springs,
the lakes and the streams.
His wise word carries  far
through the rivers and
throughout the seas.

Undines swimming
around the riverbend,
playing in the water,
curving like silk scarves
in the design of stained glass
with impressions of seafoam, and
wishing stones,
and peacock feathers, drenched
after sun showers.

Tossing pebbles along shorelines
and passing in between my toes
as I sink my body Into
your fluid Ecosystem.

## Hunter Moon
RescuePoetix/Susan Justiniano

Comfort lends itself as a subtle reminder
both healer and purifier,
licking through forces from under trapped dimensions

Melding of passion
layered with tokens of
moonrise and motion, peeking through dark fields

broken

True to its playful nature. graceful horizon whispering
remnants of melted glaciers
flat surfaces undulating, glistening

Releasing energy from foundations
dancing with life's vitality, celebration of abundance and creation
pulling dreams into reality

Eliciting pulse into moments of courage
liberation of instincts and inspirations of all the colors of life,
truest to its blended combination

Moons shift to fill feasts of nomadic motion

heart racing

tingling

*ALIVE!*

Raw in its very tone
feast to every sense
birthed in every movement
wild heart entranced

Hunter moon close enough to grasp
sanguine deep horizon
sense its healing, its quiet, its presence

Arawakan Nation follows feast of
mongrel and mulatto foods
no salting for the coming winter.

Mix of food known to First Nations,
*Comida del los conquistadores españoles,*
*tradiciones gastronómicas de los esclavos africanos*

*Arawakan, Borinqueno, Taino Nation*
under the eleventh moon of Creation
every being prepares spiritual path
sacred teachings and songs sustain us.

## The Groundwater
Dania Bowie

It's not a negotiation, it's a nightmare.
Quick, ongoing, stinging pain
A river of pain, a constant thrashing of water rushing up your nose,
Possessing your throat, an angry God,
Or is it a parent?

You can dream of running away.
Fast, deep, ringing pain
An ocean of pain, with salt stinging your eyes, stuffing your mouth with
                                                              cotton,
Flooding your brain, a jealous God,
Or is it just a brother?

You can imagine a future.
Short, useless, crashing pain
A lake of bottomless nothing, with mud forming over your feet, paralyzing
                                                              you,
Clinging to your toes, a desperate God,
Or is it a teacher?

You want more than this.
Long, sarcastic, arching pain
A puddle of blood, organs, labels, and pins, dripping from you and from the
                                                      things you did,
Itching in your chest, an unloved God,
Or is it a lover?

You decided to do something different.
Hot, steady, throbbing pain
A luscious whirlpool, instructing Ujjayi Pranayama, scratching at your throat,
Waiting for an answer while you pray, a silent God,
Or just a system?

You learned how to breathe.
Slow, tender, dulling pain

A groundwater, witnessing the glitter of the white water, hearing the reasons
rushing,

Sitting on the edge as you watch, a screaming God,
But it is you.

Artwork: *Autumn* by Brooke Bolduc "Buff Cat"

## Autumn
Brooke Bolduc

When the leaves fall I remember you
All things die, you once said

I never imagined that included you,
We are like the trees, you said

But like a tree you felt ever present. Forever standing. Timeless.

I'm in my winter and you're in your spring dear one, you whispered

I couldn't fathom that our spring would become winter.

I cried, for all things must die.

Even you, my mighty oak.

## October Leaving
Ebbie Russell

This time last year
I went into the woods in a so-called Plainfield
to stare / sob at a tree
and cry,
   "Who will hold me when I return?"

The week was
Magical, full of meaning making
time spent among
Black, brown, mostly queer kin
Heart heavy,
I questioned my return to a
Relationship that didn't feed me.

I wasn't ready

The tree with her fallen leaves
and the fallen leaves of trees around her
held me in my grief

on this Nipmuck, Pocumtuc and Wabanaki Confederacy land
where I could just be
no resistance
just rest
and weaving
I made myself
seen

**Bare**
Chyncia Smith

Though you are bare now,
There is still much to behold.
Fall tells the story
Spring was waiting to unfold.

Your branches once bud
With colors and life,
And beauty so smooth
It cut like a knife,
Into the attention of onlookers
And those passing by,
Tempting each one to wave
As new growth drew nigh.

The leaves and the flowers,
And all the things that bloom,
Pushed their way on the scene,
Forcing bareness to make room.

The colors began spilling,
Dripping down onto the page,
Transforming colorless winter wonderland
And setting the stage.
For summer warmth to creep in,
For the fullness we would soon see,
For the long sunshine-filled days
There would eventually be.

And as the lengthened days
Slowly shortened over time,
There was committed before us
The most unassuming crime.

The bold colors that once came,
So deep and so strong,

Bowed their heads singing
What would be their final song.

They bid us farewell,
Changing, their leaves falling.
They listened to the new season
Whose voice began calling.

You and other trees,
Once so rich, full, and proud.
Now empty before us,
No longer endowed,
With the brightness and life
That we held so dear.
Proof warmth has gone
And something else is near.

As you stand before me,
You are different, yet the same.
The leaves that adorned you,
Adding much to your fame,
Now paint the ground like a brush
Cluttering and canvasing the floor.
The earth looks rich
While your limbs look poor.

The bareness of your branches
Reflect a sweet memory.
It speaks to what was,
And what will one day again be.

There is so much hope,
Despite the grief,
And difficulty there is
Saying goodbye to each leaf.

Beauty remains,
No matter the season.
Growth is lovely,
No matter the reason.
Goodbye can be hard,
In that there is no shame.
Life is a given gift,
Just be glad it came.

Though you are bare now,
There is still much to behold.
Fall tells the story
Spring was waiting to unfold.

## Nonet for a Stray
Jason Montgomery

In the woods behind my house there lives
a stray cat whose fur is snow white
Not like the first winter snow
more like four day old snow
matted, and cracked gray
with bits of grass
showing through
with hope
Lost.

**Colors you see at 615am in Maine during the winter**
Sett Vincent

A dull, waterlogged blue sky - not depressed, but not motivated to pull the sun awake

The trees still black, suggestions of nature

Faded, flickering orange cream street lights that my grandfather's grandfather probably helped install

Headlights of cars and trucks - maybe working, maybe on their way to work; there's an air of that old school sense of self respect that only comes from giving your sunlight to an employer who won't remember your name

But it's calm. I'm calm. There're no birds to sing us songs of certainty, we just know the day has started. But Maine's willing to wait for you- Maine will wait for you.

## To Bear Fruits of Breath
Miriam Uduebor

Seeding
A tiny pollenated particle of potential
buried deep in darkness and pressures
seemingly without sense of direction
yet triumphantly pushing through the energizing soot
knowing this time of dormancy was only temporary,
a restful recharging, for bountiful things to come…

Rooting
Digits digging deep into the dirt
holding on for dear life
refreshed by the soothing soil
strengthened by streams from skies' toil
linking to other green and brown beings
that encourage the same

Branching
Stretching out towards the warming rays
reaching slowly and onward into the universe
as there is no limit to how far to expand
hands opened to heaven's gifts
giving and receiving through these leaves
that both leave and come again

Leafing
The lightly bound color changing pages
of nature's life cycle
inhaling and exhaling towards new life's beginning
and though drenched and dripping in times of drizzle,
when seasons change
they burst into flames that do not burn

## A Snail Primer
Mihku Paul

Carry your home on your back.
Do not hurry.
Reach toward new sensory experiences.
Sacrifice moisture to move your body forward.
Leave a trace of your passing.
Explore new surroundings whenever possible.
Travel aligned in relevant time.
Seal yourself in when necessary.
Wait for more hospitable circumstances.
Ingest all nourishment slowly.
Live as you are meant to live.
Live.
Live.

# Authors' Biographies

**Samaa Abdurraqib** lives in Wabanaki territory, close to the ocean and the mountains. Recently, her poetry can be found in *Enough! Poems of Resistance and Protest*, *Bigger Than Bravery: Black Resilience and Reclamation in a Time of Pandemic*, *Cider Press Review*, *Writing the Land: Maine*, and in her self-published chapbook *Each Day Is Like an Anchor* (2020).

**Winston Antoine**, aka Tony, is a Maine resident and Bowdoin college graduate who is originally from Baltimore. He spends his free time engaging with nature and languages. He is a true outdoorsman who engages in hunting, foraging, fishing, and gardening. Throughout his life, when he finds the time, he is an artist with words and gifts from the environment. He occasionally writes poetry and makes works of art from shells, mushrooms and bones.

**Brooke Bolduc (Artbybuffcat)** is a Black creator specializing in illustration, painting, digital art and storytelling. My goal as an artist is to share and create stories that give LGBTQ and BIPOC experiences visibility. I was born and raised in Portland and I like to support local projects that celebrate diversity and build community. Instagram: @Artbybuffcat, @Buffcatforever Facebook: Art By Buff Cat

**Dania Bowie (she/they**) is the child of Filipino immigrants who came to America during 1980s. Her art explores her experience with intergenerational trauma and healing. She paints and writes poetry, as well as short stories. She lives in Maine with her partner and two cats that are definitely people. Her work is primarily in gender, racial, and economic justice for everyone through a learning abolitionist lens.

**Samara Cole Doyon** is a second generation Haitian American from Maine—a region of unceded Wabanaki / Abenaki territory where half the roots of her family tree reside. She holds a BA in English, with graduate-level teacher training from the University of Southern Maine. She's an award-winning children's book author whose titles include *Magnificent Homespun Brown* (Tilbury House, 2020) and *Magic Like That* (Lee & Low Books, 2021). She lives with her husband, two children, and rescue pup.

**Nourish Cruz** was born and raised in New Jersey. She identifies as a Latina and is a proud member of the LBGTQ+ community. She began her journey into poetry at the age of 11 then started a successful transition into Spoken Word and Poetry Slam Competitions at the age of 15. Nourish is a board member and volunteer at A.C.P Arts, a non-profit that promotes diversity and awareness of social challenges by artistic expression, and author of "Who Shot the Rose" which touches on an array of social issues and topics of the heart.

**Crystal Davis** is a multidisciplinary and mixed media performance artist, poet, painter, freelance writer, editor, and social media marketer. She was born and raised in Jersey City, New Jersey and is the author and creator at Crystal Letters (CL), and the Co-Founder and Co-Producer of OpenRoad Poetry (ORP). She has collaborated with arts non-profit organizations and artists nationally, and internationally. Her work is inspired by nature, color, and the utilization of practical craft through art in the visual and written form.

**Dr. Deidra Suwanee Dees** and family descend from *Hotvlkvlke* (Wind Clan) and follow Muscogee stompdance traditions. Dr. Dees is author of the chapbook, *Vision Lines: Native American Decolonizing Literature.* She serves as Director/Tribal Archivist at the Poarch Band of Creek Indians. She teaches Native American Studies at the University of South Alabama. A Cornell and Harvard graduate, she writes for *Creek Corner Magazine.*

**Ashini J. Desai**, an Indian-American, was raised in NY and NJ, and lives in Pennsylvania balancing creative writing with a family and a technology career. She is co-founder/editor of Dandelion Revolution Press; and her stories and poems are published in the anthologies *Not Quite As You Were Told*, *The Secrets We Keep*, *Every Breath Alight*, *Cities*, *Overplay/Underdone*, *Word Masala*, *Yellow as Turmeric*, *Fragrant as Cloves,* and in *River Poets Journal*, *Philadelphia Poets*, and *Thema.* AshiniPoetryBlogspot.com and Instagram @AshiniWrites.

**Ian-Khara Ellasante** (they/them) is a Black, queer, trans-nonbinary poet and cultural studies scholar. A VONA alum, Cave Canem Fellow, and recipient of the New Millennium Award for Poetry, Ian-Khara has published their creative writing in *We Want It All: An Anthology of Radical Trans Poetics, PipeWrench, The Feminist Wire, The Volta*, and elsewhere. Their critical writing has appeared in *Ethnic and Racial Studies* and *Transgender Studies Quarterly.* Ian-Khara teaches at Bates College.

**Joy George** (she/her) is a facilitator, organizer, healer, writer and researcher. Born and raised in the Bronx as a daughter and sister of Nigerian diaspora, Joy researches racial trauma, healing modalities and resilience building, and facilitates transformative processes in the US and around the world. She holds a BA in Political Science and Black Studies from Swarthmore College, has facilitated a number of Jams with YES!, and after living and working in Maine, now breathes life into the Restore Oakland team in the Bay Area, California.

**Robert Anthony Gibbons** has been nominated for a Pushcart and published in hundreds of literary magazines and in several anthologies. Recent publications include: *Killens Review, Tribes, Involuntary Magazine, Peregrine, Expound, Promethean, Turtle Island Quarterly, KillerWhale,* and *Suisun Valley Review, Voices of Lefferts* and the *Bronx Memoir Project: Vol. 2*. Robert's first collection is *Close to the Tree* (Three Rooms Press, 2012), and his chapbook is *Flight* (Poets Wear Prada, 2019).

**Myronn Hardy** is the author of the forthcoming *Aurora Americana* (Princeton University Press). His poems have appeared in *The New York Times Magazine, POETRY Magazine, The New Republic, The Georgia Review,* and elsewhere. He teaches at Bates College.

**Julia S. Jordan-Zachery** is professor and chair of the Women's Gender and Sexuality Studies Department at Wake Forest University. She is the author of the award-winning book *Black Women, Cultural Images and Social Policy, Shadow Bodies: Black Women, Ideology, Representation, and Politics,* and *Erotic Testimonies: Black Women Daring to be Wild and Free,* and several edited volumes. She produced the documentary *Healing Roots* and the chapbook, *Eat the Meat and Spit out the Bones.*

**Rheros Iliad Kagoni** is a queer, non-binary, Black individual living in Southern Maine. A Mainer at heart, Rheros Iliad has finished their Psychology degree and is trying to figure out what it means to be a grown-up, with a "grown-up" job. Although they don't consider themselves to be a poet, everyone Rheros knows would say otherwise. You can find them on Instagram and Facebook @thatmainepoet . Rheros also hates writing bios about themself.

**JuPong Lin** makes art, poetry, community, and ceremony to honor our Beloved Earth and all her critters. Ghosts of her born-place, Taiwan, haunt her to reconnect with her ancestors, human and nonhuman. Currently living in Nonotuck/Nipmuc Land, Amherst, Massachusetts, she blends paper-folding, poetics, and storycircle to co-create spaces for the sacred work of transforming harm. JuPong is faculty of the Interdisciplinary Arts program at Goddard College and a PhD candidate in Environmental Studies at Antioch University.

**Jason R. Montgomery** is a Chicano/Indigenous Californian activist, writer, painter, and playwright from El Centro, California. He currently lives in Holyoke, Massachusetts. In 2016 Jason co-founded the arts activism collective Attack Bear Press and in 2020 he founded 50 Arrow Gallery. Along with Alexandra Woolner, Jason is 2021-2023 Easthampton Poets Laureate.

**Mihku Paul** is a Wolastoqey writer, activist and multidisciplinary creative born and raised in Maine. She is an enrolled member of Kingsclear First Nation, N.B. Canada. Mihku holds an MFA from the Stonecoast Creative Writing Program. Her work encompasses poetry, graphic art and mixed media including recordings of poetry spoken in her native dialect. She has been published in numerous anthologies, and her chapbook is *20th Century PowWow Playland*.

**RescuePoetix | Susan Justiniano** is the first Puerto Rican woman Poet Laureate of Jersey City, NJ (2020-2022) and State of New Jersey Beat Poet Laureate (2022-2024), a bilingual globally published performing poet, advocate, spoken word artist, recording artist and teaching artist. She established RescuePoetix™ and is an arts advocate deeply involved in the arts community since 2006 and currently serves on the boards of several arts organizations throughout the USA. https://linktr.ee/rescuepoetix

**Dylan Richmond** is a senior at Bowdoin College majoring in Dance and English. Raised in Connecticut, he has received state-wide recognition for his speech at a BLM march in 2020. Dylan is a Mellon Mays Fellow with a research focus in Black embodiment and performance and plans to enter graduate school to diversify and decolonize academia. He values his achievements leading a poetry club, his volleyball team, and his work with the Bowdoin College Art Museum. Dylan also enjoys petting large dogs.

**Ebbie Russell**, a U.S.-born Black queer femme, is a self-taught artist whose writing, choreography, and visual art is heavily rooted in African diasporic movements, belief in time travel, and exploration of how dance can address, heal, and honor intergenerational trauma and chronic illness. Ebbie is also a teaching artist who designs zines and workshops with young people and community members in and around western Massachusetts.

**Chyncia Smith**, a New Jersey resident and Bucknell University alumna, loves writing and mentoring student-athletes. She is a person who stutters and joyously appreciates meeting others with the same special trait. Chyncia is constantly in awe of God's power and beauty in creation. She has an adventurous spirit and outside is one of her favorite places to be. She is a CPA, a volunteer Outdoor Afro leader and loves learning about her African American heritage.

**Miriam "Myri" Uduebor (they/them & she/her)** is a Black Queer artist, learner, and healer who loves the energy, creative expression, and healing power of poetry. Traveling from Karankawa land in the South/Texas region, Myri has been living in Wabanaki/Abenaki land for almost four years and is excited to be a part of more artistic adventures in the Maine community.

**Sett Vincent (he/him)** is a mixed-race youth of color who moved to Maine from Connecticut who talks openly about his Autism, his experiences of not finishing high school, and being born into poverty. His work is focused on finding systems of harm and replacing them with care, and connecting with people as whole human beings. His humanity is focused on building community, knitting, and creating art that helps him process the world around him.

**Maya Williams (ey/they/she)** is a religious Black multiracial nonbinary suicide survivor who is currently the poet laureate of Portland, Maine. Maya was also one of three artists of color selected to represent Maine in The Kennedy Center's *Arts Across America* series. Ey has published poems in venues such as *FreezeRay*, *glitterMOB*, *The Portland Press Herald*, *The Coop*, *Indianapolis Review*, and more. You can find more of their work at mayawilliamspoet.com.

# About the Editor and Foreword Writer

Samaa Abdurraqib,
Editor

**Samaa Abdurraqib, PhD** lives in Wabanaki territory, close to the ocean and the mountains. She is in love with the natural world and is committed to learning more about the land and life that surrounds her. She served as a volunteer leader for the national organization Outdoor Afro (2018-2022) and is currently deep into a year-long Maine Master Naturalist course. Recently, Samaa's poetry can be found in *Enough! Poems of Resistance and Protest*, *Bigger Than Bravery: Black Resilience and Reclamation in a Time of Pandemic*, *Cider Press Review*, *Writing the Land: Maine*, and in her self-published chapbook *Each Day Is Like an Anchor* (2020).

**Shanta Lee** is an award winning writer across genres, journalist, visual artist and public intellectual actively participating in the cultural discourse with work that has been widely featured. Shanta Lee is the author of poetry collections *GHETTOCLAUSTROPHOBIA: Dreamin of Mama While Trying to Speak Woman in Woke Tongues* (Diode Editions, 2021) and the illustrated poetry collection *Black Metamorphoses* (Etruscan Press, 2023). Her latest work, *Dark Goddess: An Exploration of the Sacred Feminine*, is on view at the University of Vermont's Fleming Museum of Art.    www.Shantalee.com

Photo by Liz LaVorgna

Shanta Lee,
Foreword Writer

9 781737 574064